SCHREINER

A One-woman Play

Whether performed or read, this play evokes a vivid picture
of Olive Schreiner, both as private individual and as active
public figure contending in society. She is the only protago-
nist — other powerful characters, like Cecil Rhodes and
Havelock Ellis, are around but in the wings — and the words
are historically her own, drawn almost entirely from her own
writings and seamed together by the playwright in a series
of scenes from her life's journey. Stephen Gray sees Schreiner
as always in transit:'on the Union–Castle route between London Docks and Table Bay, always coming and going, always
with great ambitions'. Within that restless ambience is projected the many-faceted, remarkable woman — passionate,
creative, prophetic — who is regarded as one of the key figures in the birth of a post-colonial South African literature.

Schreiner – A One-woman Play was premièred in the
Rhodes University Theatre on 9 July 1983 — in the year
which marks the centenary of the publication of *The Story
of an African Farm*. The play was presented by the Company
of the Market Theatre, Johannesburg, starring Elize Cawood,
directed by Lucille Gillwald.

OTHER BOOKS BY THE SAME AUTHOR

Southern African Literature: An Introduction

POEMS
It's About Time
The Assassination of Shaka (with Cecil Skotnes)
Hottentot Venus and other poems
Love Poems, Hate Poems

NOVELS
Local Colour
Visible People
Caltrop's Desire

PLAYS
An Evening at the Vernes
Cold Stone Jug

COLLECTIONS EDITED
Writers' Territory
A World of their Own
Modern South African Stories
Poems for Performance
Theatre One
Theatre Two
Athol Fugard

STEPHEN GRAY

SCHREINER

A ONE-WOMAN PLAY

Cape Town
DAVID PHILIP
Johannesburg London

SECOND IMPRESSION 1987

First published in 1983 by David Philip, Publisher (Pty) Ltd, P O Box 408, Claremont, Cape, South Africa

Distributed in the U K and Europe by Global Book Resources Ltd, 109 Great Russell Street, London WC1B 3NA

ISBN 0 908396 97 X

Typeset by Typesetting Services, Johannesburg

Printed and bound by Citadel Press, Polaris Road, Lansdowne, Cape, South Africa

CONTENTS

NOTES 1
   Olive Schreiner 1
   The script 4
   The performance 5
   The stage 7
   Scenes 8
SCHREINER – A ONE-WOMAN PLAY 9
   Part One 9
   Part Two 37

Schreiner – A One-woman Play was premièred in the Rhodes University Theatre as part of the Grahamstown Festival on 9 July 1983. The play was presented by the Company of the Market Theatre, Johannesburg, starring Elize Cawood, directed by Lucille Gillwald.

NOTES

Olive Schreiner

Born 24 March, 1855, on Wittebergen Mission Station, in the Herschel District, north-eastern Cape. One of twelve children of Gottlob Schreiner and Rebecca Lyndall. Her birth coincided with the promulgation of the Cape Parliament, whereby the Colony gained representative government, and the Xhosa so-called 'National Suicide', whereby the Eastern Border was opened up for white settlement. Most of her childhood was spent on the frontier.

With her father dismissed from the church and bankrupt, the family split up, and Olive moved from one relative to another, housekeeping, until at nineteen she could earn her living as a governess on farms near Aliwal North and Cradock. While teaching and doing domestic work, she wrote the novels *Undine, The Story of an African Farm* and a large early draft of *From Man to Man,* as well as keeping journals and writing copious letters.

With her savings, in 1881, aged twenty-six, she first escaped to Britain, ostensibly to become a doctor. The publication of *African Farm* — a century ago — in 1883 brought her fame and a modest income on which she survived for the rest of her life, both as a writer and an independent spokesperson.

In England she formed many a lifelong friendship with sociological, psychological and political reformers, including Havelock Ellis, Karl Pearson, Edward Carpenter and Eleanor Marx. She developed a complex programme of personal action that blended the principles of Freethinking, Socialism, the Women's Enfranchisement Movement and Conscientious Objection. Above all, she argued for a new relationship between man and woman in which two equal, independent beings could share — the marriage of the New Woman and the New Man. During her eight first years in England she travelled restlessly, as far afield as to Italy, engaged on her 'sex work' and producing short, prophetic dream-allegories, which enjoyed a considerable vogue.

She returned to the Cape in 1889 to face a decade of colonial politics which featured her (and her brother Will — W. P. Schreiner, later Prime Minister) as a non-aligned commentator and polemicist, systematically anti-Capitalist and pro-underdog. Based largely at Matjiesfontein, she produced the widely-published articles which were later collected as *Thoughts on South Africa*. During the Jameson Raid crisis she responded with the novella, *Trooper Peter Halket of Mashonaland* and then a stop-the-war pamphlet, *An English-South African's View of the Situation,* which is one of the first documents to define the composite South African personality which she saw as the foundation of a greater country that could be.

She was sometimes confined during the Anglo-Boer War of 1899-1902 at Hanover in the Cape under martial law, though, as a delegate from Hanover, she sat on the platform of the largest public meeting ever held in Cape Colony — where 10,000 people gathered at Worcester on 6 December, 1900 — in protest of the war. Her pro-Boer sympathies were widely publicised, and her pacifism largely overlooked.

With her as a speaker was her husband, Samuel Cronwright-Schreiner, whom she married at the age of thirty-eight in 1894 in Middelburg, Cape. Their only child was born on 30 April, 1895. Haunted by periodic attacks of asthma from the age of sixteen, Schreiner's life with Cron seems to have been recurrently shiftless and driven — in search of the right altitude, dryness, and surroundings for the sufferer. The ravages of her illness eventually led to an enlargement of the heart. Between 1902 and 1913, Schreiner and Cron lived variously in Kimberley, De Aar, Johannesburg, Cape Town and Hanover (for half a decade), and they usually visited Grahamstown and the Kowie for holidays. Her health and his life as a businessman drew them apart.

When Schreiner left for a trip to Europe in 1913 — and became marooned in England throughout World War One — she was not to see Cronwright again for seven years, and then only for a month in London. In 1920 she turned around again, this time to die.

Her last two decades were not visibly productive, though she elaborated her masterpiece, *From Man to Man*, published posthumously in 1926. Of her 'sex book' only the fragment, *Woman and Labour* was issued — mapped out in the 80s and 90s it was, when it came out in 1911, still a manifesto, a passionate appeal and a motivation which perhaps, today, is the work by which Schreiner is best remembered. She lived to see the franchise for women in Australia, but not in the U.K. or South Africa (1930 — white adults only). But *Woman and Labour* still speaks to a condition of inequality that the colonial world has passed down to us.

She died in Wynberg, alone in a boarding house, on 10 December, 1920. She left an estate of £482 — not sufficient for the funding of the scholarship she planned to endow for talented South African women. She was buried by Cronwright, with her baby and dog, in a sarcophagus on Buffel's Kop above Cradock, overlooking the farm where she had written *African Farm*.

The script
This play is drawn virtually entirely from Schreiner's recorded
words. Every line has its source. Mostly, the following are used:

> *Undine* (1929)
> *Dreams* (1891)
> *Dream Life and Real Life* (1893)
> *Thoughts on South Africa* (1923)
> *Woman and Labour* (1911)
> *The Life of Olive Schreiner* (1924)
> *The Letters of Olive Schreiner* (1924).

I owe gratitude to many biographers of Schreiner — S. C.
Cronwright, Vera Buchanan-Gould, D. L. Hobman, Richard
Rive, Ruth First and Ann Scott. Also to the following: Susan
Gardner for background material; Cherry Clayton for making
her collection of unpublished Schreiner letters available, and
other material from many collections; the National English
Literary Museum for photographic and journal material.
Especially helpful has been the article, "A Voyage with Olive
Schreiner" by Rev R. E. Welsh (1894).

I have taken the view that Schreiner's life was neither that of
a child-like colonial genius, at one extreme, nor that of an
overstrained neurotic prophet and failure, at the other.
Schreiner is shown here as a transitional Victorian figure in
whom the issues of the modern world were in the making;
subsidiary to this, she was also the first to articulate a post-
colonial sensibility in the South African context.

Two of her sayings have guided me — one from Emerson,
one of her own:

"The life of man is the true romance, which, when it is
valiantly conducted, will yield the imagination a higher joy
than any fiction."

"There can be no *absolutely true* life of anyone except written
by themselves and then only if written from the eye of God."

The performance
This is a play; not a reading.

It is important not only that Schreiner be listened to, but
watched. No passage in the following script is merely a
sequence of words, though its source might well have been. I
have always set a passage in a framing context which is at odds
with the drift of the text — what appears solemn and
sanctimonious might, in fact, be mockery; what appears
sentimental and forgiving might be relentless and angry. It is in
the gap between the text and this sub-text that the power lies.
We must hear one thing, see that its effect or its truth is
different. This is not merely to demonstrate that Schreiner was
a contradictory personality, but to complicate issues which
would otherwise be cut-and-dried, to give the reality to the
struggle of life in the making.

A sense of this reality may be achieved in two ways. Firstly,
the performer is working with micro-realistic details — a
nervous gesture repeated, an ill-timed pause, a spurt of irrita-
tion can betray what is behind a cool, confident exterior; an
ironic edge — the tendency to send herself up — is always
present, even when she is most tendentious. We must realise
soon that it is not the story that counts, but the moment of its
invention; not the conclusion, but the route followed. The
words Schreiner wrote — in this selection they are all covertly
autobiographical — were but the nets thrown about personal
issues. Often she throws the net in one direction only for us to
realise the issue is in quite another direction. This playfulness
with truth can be brought about with complex body language,
with subliminal suggestiveness, by concentrating on the gap
between the supposed and the true.

Secondly, this play should also appear to have the power of
being self-inventing. This can be achieved by using the Brechtian technique of never letting the performer forget that she is
within the play at the same time as she is making it. We must
always feel she knows why she is presenting us something —
that this is a public performance, in a theatre, in our own time.
If she falters in this long script, that would be no disgrace; it
could be an advantage — she could refer to the script to remind
herself, and us, where she is. With good humour. There are
brief passages here where the performer can, and must, be
herself when stepping out of character; those can be improvised
further according to the occasion. This double perspective is

there to achieve the Brechtian effect: to make an audience be entertained, while thinking why it is being entertained. We are watching not only one performance, but experiencing an encounter between then and now.

To emphasize the play-like effect of this script, the overall story has been broken into many fragments, arranged in achronological sequence. This is to dispense with linear narrative to a large extent, in favour of a cross-referring structure that zigzags forwards and backwards. We see her life in nine segments, each segment related to the overall metaphor of the to-and-fro voyage. Schreiner herself dispensed with progressively developmental narrative early in her career, so the technique used here is appropriate to her: she believed not that a work should set forth with only one destination in mind, but that the deepening of the moment contained its own answer. She was engaged in achieving a refinement of the sensibility, not in slick transformations and easy denouements.

So, this script is built like a puzzle of various pieces, and each piece throws a new light on the same portrait. We cannot see the whole until the last piece is in place but, even then, not until we simultaneously recall them all. To avoid a too superficial judgement forming, I have always arrested a scene just before it jells, and cut to a contrasting scene, and to another contrasting scene after that.

But the performance should remain seamless, interrupted by jump cuts that are as speedy as possible. The titles of scenes should be projected.

The stage
No set is necessary.

One tin trunk covered in labels, in which Schreiner stores her life, and the performer her props.

Two deck-chairs, ship's style; one writing desk; a hat-stand on which all the garments used for changes are visible.

Scenes

Part One
1. September, 1897 — London to Cape Town

2. March, 1881 — *Kinfauns Castle* — Port Elizabeth to London
("Dream Life and Real Life", "I Thought I Stood")

3. October, 1889 — *Norham Castle* — London to Cape Town
("The Nurse's Story" from *Undine*)

4. 1891 — Cape Town
("The Woman's Rose", "The Salvation of a Ministry")

Part Two
5. December, 1913 — *Edinburgh Castle* — Cape Town to London
(*Woman and Labour*)

6. 1903 — Cape Town to Port Elizabeth

7. January, 1897 — *Dunvegan Castle* — Cape Town to London

8. October, 1887 — London to Basle Express

9. August, 1920 — *Balmoral Castle* — London to Cape Town

PART ONE

1. September, 1897 — London to Cape Town
(Mode: Interview)

A performer playing Olive Schreiner, in her early forties. She wears her black dress with white cuffs, and an ornate, floppy hat and gloves. She is brisk, forthright, a bit nervous.
... Well, as you can see, I'm in perfect health. Yes, a sea voyage... yes, yes, Sanatogen. You can't advertise in your magazine. Off the record, I practically live on Sanatogen. Well, I can't give you very long — my husband will be here; he's opening the telegrams. A deck cabin, yes, otherwise — well, I do get the old heavy breathing, pure, pure agony. So, what is it you wish to know? I don't normally consent to give interviews...

Surely that's on record. No, forty-three. If you mean, am I past child-bearing, ach, not quite is the answer. Though children are a bit past being borne by me — Not you, child, I meant... I did, once, have a child, under my heart in a lead-lined coffin. She lived sixteen hours. I cradled her in my arms for another ten... Joy and grief in one day.

My own childhood, yes, but I've written about little else, you know... in the African Karoo, yes... desert, yes... What the British don't know about their Empire would fill many more volumes than that.

Oh, absolutely authentic. You are listening to a truly South African accent. I can even drop a few words of the Taal, like agteros and voorlaaier... Well, the agteros, you see, is the last one of a pair in a team, and the voorlaaier — you load it from the front. The other way round you'd have a vooros and — an agterlaaier wouldn't really work — pull the trigger and it goes up in your face... Do they intend to use them? — well, wouldn't you? If the greatest empire the world has ever known, on which the sun and moon never set, was coming to dig you over for money?

... That hardly means I'm anti-British. I'm against the use of force... yes, in *any* circumstances... No, we are held to Britain by a network of tender bonds, a tough cable of affection stretching across six thousand miles of sea. Yet we are distinct, like a crew all in the same ship. We've set out on our own

9

voyage together; all South Africans are united by that very
venture...

No, we are bonded by our very mixture of races itself. You
take a typical Cape household. The father is an Englishman.
The mother a so-called Boer — half Dutch and half French,
with a French name. The children are all three. Their governess
is, well, German. The cook is a Half-caste, partly Boer, partly
slave. The housemaid is a Half-caste, partly Hottentot, father,
oh yes, an English soldier — there is a lot of co-habitation. The
man who cleans the boots is a Xhosa. The groom Basuto, left
over from the wars. A plum-pudding, my dear. All in the same
boat...

Yes, they're giving lectures on me now... I am the national
literature! I've never been to school, you know; not had sixpence spent on my education. I sometimes felt bitter when I
thought of the advantages others had; I don't know. When
people say it's unnatural for Lyndall and Waldo to have such
thoughts, oh, I laugh to myself. Yes, you can teach yourself
everything, but it's at such a fearful loss of strength. I'm sorry I
never had any help. You did, ah good. You see, look where you
are now. You don't have to be self-made anymore.

Do I dream a lot — what kind of question's that? Er, of
course that's what we live by. Men will die for it. But they're
hardly dreams when they hold up to the light of day. Are they?
Don't you dare make out I'm some impractical, vacant female
rhapsodist when what I say, and what I do, is what moves
millions of men and billions of pounds sterling!

... Next major work? Well... *African Farm* was fifteen years
ago... yes, one does get sunk by an early success. No, I couldn't
go back and read it now. But there is my new little success, yes,
Trooper Peter — oh you must, it's in quite a cheap edition...
mightier than the sword, yes... well, nothing'll make up for the
personal damage it's caused my family and myself ... my poor
mother's eighty. There's my brother Will you know of, no,
Attorney-General, dear. I have another brother and sister and
— of course Cron — C.R.O.N. wright-hyphen-Schreiner, and
there's *his* family. You might say the war will be cutting up our
plum-pudding... No, as long as the porthole's open; there's an
ashtray... just blow it the other way.

Well, no. I have seen — what happened with us in two
hundred years — happen in two hundred days, in Mashonaland. I know, I've lived through three Kaffir Wars... Don't

believe it; colonization is liquor and guns. You don't civilise a man by hanging him! There's a curious property of blood shed on the scaffold for political offences; it doesn't dry up...

Try and understand there weren't the opportunities open to us when I was your age — governess, nurse, and that was it. Woman reporter —they'd never heard of such a thing. No, only asthma, dear, means you can't inhale and I go all splotchy; blow it that way. Not now, my husband thinks it's bad for me.

Relationships to men?... next question... How forward you are.

When did I first? — oh, travel, travel. Eases the pain... I get terribly — can't breathe or — I'm dreading the Tropics. Gets worse as you get older. Me? — deck-quoits in these awful clothes! I would die of laughter! Next!

Ah, you have done your homework. Not a shred of truth in it — English as you are. Someone called me a German halfbreed, but my father, you know, was a little German shoemaker. Went out from Switzerland for the London Missionary Society, from here, please note — yes, Uncle Otto — and he always talked and wrote to us in English. Apart from agterlaaier and vooros I know no... little French, little Dutch. Not enough to get my head blown off, yes!

No no, I've been called far worse: white Hottentot, for instance! and Jew — oh... oh I'm sorry. Never have spotted it — on my mother's side there's supposed to be, which accounts for the dark eyes, but I think I made that up!

Have terrible difficulty distinguishing between fact and fiction; all creative people do; I think... ah, do you like it? — I used to wear it down my back and tread on it. Now it's falling out in clumps, look at that. In Africa I always keep a hat on. Very dry for the skin, raging sun. Do you know that when I was a child I used to wear a kappie, so *(Face wizened like a Buddha's)*... oh, my baby girl, my baby girl; you know, I lay there cradling her for ten hours, singing to her — just a gentle lullaby... I do that sometimes.

Not at all! Same thing! Birth and death, they're the same. I'll tell you but it'll make you scared. But what a culture, that makes such a stink about dying, when it's the most natural thing in the world. You just open your arms and let him come... What beautiful things I think of Death. He is always beautiful — snow-white, with huge silver wings and he smiles down and folds you up... like a mother duckling...

11

Yes, hard to breathe with all those feathers! Ach, but who could possibly be afraid of yielding to a force like that? Not morbid, my dear — it's society's morbid. The times we live in.

I used to think so, yes — but what? — what? — I've miscarried four times, and I can tell you it's hell. You feel so weak. I sat on the beach, drained, staring at the waves, and I said out loud, who made a woman's lot? We know who made men, don't we, but there were many devils around when He devised us...

Then you should. It's every woman's right over the age of thirty. For your health and bodily functions. No, you don't need a husband. I didn't say... no, no, if you find some suitable man. No, to hell with marriage. Motherhood can only do good. They don't care for them very much... Well, if you can find some nice journalist for whom fatherhood... don't quote me on this. Put up your pen! Now, don't you dare quote one word of what I'm going to tell you. Put it away and forget I ever mentioned it... Oh, don't have another because my husband is coming. Ah, look at you, your hopeful eyes, your ivory hand shaking... now, now, put your hand on my knee, there, there... *(Taking a glove off, stroking her)*

Now, if you're going to be a professional woman, be an example to all women, and to all men. You've smashed your chains, but now you must learn how to walk. You've found your voice, but now you must learn how to speak. Forget your silly questions: who cares how the Duchess of so-and-so furnishes her house? Who cares how an authoress like me talks and plays golf? I never go into a railway station and see women's literature there but my heart sinks. We women demand the franchise. It's not the men who can enfranchise us, but we — we must enfranchise ourselves. We must free ourselves from the mean and trivial. It eats at our women's souls. Every woman who does good, able and balanced work aids the standing of all women, more even than she could do by working for the vote.

Wouldn't it be better for you to write a paper on — the duties of the women of a dominant race? Say in Africa, where at present we do dominate, oh yes. Turn your thoughts away from those trivial, trivial... Look to literature to free us from that. Who cares about my dowdy, awful black dress — I was married in it, and I'll go to my grave in it, and I love it. I mourn like our dreary Queen, for a world that cannot work. Give us labour and the training which fits us for labour! We demand this, not for ourselves alone, but for the race! No, sh! sh! you're a bright girl and you'll go far. Your turn is now. Doesn't matter if you're Jewish... *(The girl returns to her seat)* I'm sorry I don't have any tea. Um, it's not my ship!

But you ask me two simple questions: How were you educated? I've told you I never went to any school like you. But to give you the true story would mean rending my heart open before you. I'd have to describe the most sacred and beautiful hours of my private life. The books I loved and studied, the scenes I visited. The influence of a thousand, thousand beneficent things, so sacred, so intimate I'd not open them to my closest friend. And you wish to blazon all that around every newspaper stall.

And you ask me why I wrote *African Farm.* That's easier. But do you think a reader with sixpence really wants to know? — when even those infinite powers of existence which shape human life perhaps don't know. From the first day I can remember, I've made stories — and poems — and plays — and essays. And shall do, till the breath goes out of my body.

All right, ask me why I printed *African Farm.* To help others. So that I could share my loneliness. Of the things I've made since then, I have not written down half. Of those I've written, but one or two have been printed. I hope some soul who reads them finds joy in them. Though the hundredth part of the writer's joy can never be known, my child. There now, don't think me unkind...

Now, do me an article on the Woman Question by Monday. Post it to me in the African desert. Just put Olive Schreiner, De Aar. Ah, the blast, up goes the gangway... Your cigarettes and your pad — yes, yes, oh do get out! Don't think me unkind ... Yes, thank you. Share my loneliness... Goodbye...

As she waves her imaginary guest out, the lights fade. She is at the hat-stand to deposit her hat and gloves, and let down her hair.

2. March, 1881 — *Kinfauns Castle* – Port Elizabeth to London
(Mode: Lesson)

She has long black hair down her back; youthful, angular, aggressive.

Yes, listen. I am all of twenty-six now. I am on board ship for the very first time. Not so luxurious. I live on an allowance from my brother, Theo. I'm going to visit my brother, Fred, in England. The fare I paid for myself. That's the official story. My portmanteau is full of manuscripts — three novels, many stories. *(Claps her right hand in her left palm)* Ach, I have this habit of walking and clapping my hands, composing as I go — not so easy in a confined space. My mother used to thrash me for saying 'Ach.' Ach, ach, I can say it as much as I like. *(The following sequence is performed striding intermittently between steel walls)*

Listen carefully because — Miss Olive's going to talk very fast and very softly, so put anything that can drop with a clatter — on the floor — your slates, handbags — put it down, your programme, sir, etc. Right *(Clap)*, here it is: "A Little African Story."

There once was a little girl — no, pay attention! Put it away, you're not at home... Once upon a time there was... a girl, called *(Inventing: tensely)* Jannita. And she lived in the Karoo — you all know the Karoo, milk-bushes, and red sand, and thorny acacia. Milk-bush is the one like a bundle of green rods. Yes, around Leliekloof, where I used to walk up and down.

Jannita. The plain stretched before her, as the ocean does before me now. She would moon, and sit, and look at it, while around her were — Angora goats. She was herding them, like curly waves. But Jannita, you see, was not happy — *(Aside)* like all my children she was miserable. Crying great drops. By and by she was so exhausted, and the sun so hot, she laid her head against the milk-bush — and dropped off asleep.

And she dreamed a beautiful dream. Remember how we used to, out of sheer longing. She dreamed that, when she went back to the farmhouse, the walls were just — covered with vines and roses. And the fat old Boer, to whom she was indentured, smiled at her, for once. And the stick he held across the gateway — for the goats to jump over — was a lily rod. When she went to the kitchen door, her mistress took off her straw hat — and gave her a whole roosterkoek. And the daughter came up and gave her — a handful of blue flowers. And the suitor was there; when she pulled off his boots, he didn't give her a kick — he said: "Ik hebt u lief," you know. It was a beautiful, impossible dream. But she insisted on dreaming it.

One of the wavy goats came up and licked her cheek. And she dreamed it was her father. He said, "I was only asleep that day, when I lay under the thorn-bush." They were itinerants, so she was stranded; not easy for a young coloured girl. He asked her in this dream why her feet were bare, what the marks on her limbs were. Then he picked her up, and put her head on his shoulder, and carried her away, away! She laughed, very nervous — she could feel his beard. His arms were so strong.

As she lay there dreaming, a Hottentot shepherd came up to her. He was dressed in ragged yellow trousers. He looked at the little girl lying in the hot sun. Then he walked off, and caught one of the fattest Angoras, and held its mouth fast as he stuck it under his arm. He looked back to see she was still asleep, and jumped down into one of the sluits. Then came to an overhanging bank. There were two other men there. One was a tiny ragged old Bushman, the kind you don't see anymore. The other was an English navvy, in a dark blue blouse. They propped up the goat and the navvy took out his knife and drove it in. The blood spurted all over his blouse — don't feel faint, it gets worse! *(Calling attention)* All right, children — he dug the knife in, and the little kid squirmed around — and then — its head fell over. They skinned it, and buried the entrails. The Hottentot man put a leg under his coat and walked away, leaving the rest for the other two.

When little Johanna awoke — I mean Janna, Jannita — she awoke, and it was almost sunset. She sat up, very frightened, but her goats were all about her. She began to drive them home, as sure as could be that none were lost. Dirk the Hottentot stood at the kraal door in his ragged yellow trousers; he'd already brought his flock back. The fat old Boer put his stick across the gate. Her mistress shooed the goats in with her apron. The daughter watched and the suitor counted. Dirk the Hottentot was counting, and Jannita counted. Ses-en-twintig, sewe-en-twintig. . . You can use this story instead of bromide. Except, it'll keep you awake. Ag-en-twintig. . . Then little Jannita knew what was coming.

"Have you been to sleep today?" said the old Boer. "There is one missing."

"Ja, the little one with the crumpled ear," said the mistress.

"Ja," said Dirk the Hottentot.

"Hoekom, is it dood?" said the daughter, and the suitor said a leopard must have eaten it.

"Have you been dreaming?" said the old Boer.

Jannella said in a low voice: "Nee baas," and then she felt that deadly sickness when you tell a lie, and she said: "Ja baas."

"Do you think you'll have any supper this evening?" said the old Boer.

"No," said Jannola.

"What do think you will have?"

"I don't know," she said.

And the mother and the daughter and the suitor went back to the farmhouse... *(She brings her fist down in crashes)*

"Give me your whip," said the Boer to Dirk the Hottentot.

There — there must be a moral — don't you dream when you should be attentive! Pay attention! Ach, but those were terrible days — I can hear the lash coming down on that child; hear her moan and writhe and... If an angel should gather up in his cup all the tears that have been shed, the bitterest would be those of children — children forced to be old before their time... I was put out to housekeep, then teach. But I was never a poor coloured. Well, there she is, flayed alive. There is a sequel.

The moon was full that night, a troublesome, damaging time. The little girl crept to the door of the outhouse and gazed at the moon. When you are hungry and rigid with pain, you do not cry. She stared across the plain at the sand, and the low karoo-bushes with the moonlight on them, and drove her hands between her thighs. The one palm was cut right open, and she wound it in her pinafore.

And then, before she knew it, she was running away towards the moon. Away, away, anywhere but on that farm. At last her legs began to tremble under her, and she stopped to breathe. The house was a speck behind her. She dropped on the earth and held her panicking sides, and she felt guilty. And she began to think now: if she stayed on the plain, they would trace her footsteps in the morning. But if she made for the river, waded deep into the water, they would not find her prints. She decided — the river.

But the water in the river was low; just a scum of silver on the broad bed of sand. She could not dive, swim, immerse. She stepped into it and bathed her hands in the delicious cold water, and waited until she was sure she could hear no more.

Then up and up the stream she walked where it rattled over the pebbles, up past where the farmhouse lay. And where the rocks were large, she leaped over, one to another. The night wind in her face made her strong. She had never felt such a breeze before. So the night smells to the wild animals, because they are free. A free thing feels as a chained never can.

At last she came to the place where the willows grew. She could not tell why, she could not tell the reason, but a feeling of fear came over her. It was the bank she had seen in her dream, and now there was a fire burning, under the overhanging place. Exactly the place, but it was night.

She thought for a moment it was her father, boiling his coffee-pot. He used to do that, when they first trekked into that district. Then he asked the old Boer for work. And the mistress set her to sewing and darning in the kitchen doorway, when her father looked after the goats. If it were him, she'd throw herself on his back and they'd fly, fly away. But that was in dream life. What she saw now was real life.

The moon shone through the branches. She drew them apart and made a small opening with her poor, sore fingers. A little old-fashioned Bushman sat over some burning coals, braaiing the meat. Stretched on the ground was an Englishman, dressed in a blouse, with a heavy, but alert face. On the stone beside him was none other than Dirk the Hottentot, cleaning his bowie knife. And she listened to every word they said; she could hear it all.

"You take all the money," said the Bushman.

"But you take the cask of brandy," said the Englishman.

"I will set the roof alight, in six places," said the Bushman. "That I will do, because a Dutchman burnt my mother once, alive in a hut, with three brothers of mine!"

"And I drive the goats into the mountains," said Dirk.

"You are sure there is no one else on the farm?" said the navvy.

"I've told you," said Dirk, "the two natives have gone to town with the suitor; the maids have gone to the dance; there is only the old man and the mistress and the daughter."

"But suppose," said the navvy, "he has the gun at his bed-side."

"Never," said Dirk, "it hangs in the passage, and the cartridges."

"And the little coloured girl, what about her?" said the navvy.

"But she is drowned already," said Dirk. "We followed her tracks to the water's edge, and the great pool has no bottom."

"Poor thing," snorted the Englishman. "She must have had no reason to like the Boer."

She listened to every word, and they talked on.

Then the Bushman sat up. A Bushman's ear is so fine he knows a jackal's tread from a wild dog's. "Ha, what is that?" he said. *(Pause)*

"I heard nothing," said the navvy. "Finish your meat."

Said Dirk, "It's only a dassie."

"No dassie, no dassie," said the Bushman, "see, what is there, moving under the willows?"

The wind blew the branches aside and little Jannina lay still, still.

Then the league of three made ready to attack the farmhouse and kill the three Bears, I mean — the three Boers. So, you have a dilemma for our girl. She is safe, presumed dead. She has every reason not to want to help Mr Bear and Mrs Bear and especially Daughter Bear. And she's hungry, remember, and tired and sore, covered in blood. What can she do?...

No, she's the kind of child who could live in the wilds, that's the whole point. She could make a pantry of the wild plants, and snuggle into a shelter; to her the veld is just the place. But she can actually see the farmhouse now, with its low roof and the kraals and the windmill pumping, pumping. And the three are setting off. What can she do?

(Relaxing) Well, you must know what she tried to do. And you must know there were two roads to the homestead. One went along the open veld, the shortest; but you'd be seen half a mile off. The other went along the river bank under rocks and trees. The little figure ran on and on, never looking, never thinking. There where the road was thickest, there over the open space, there through the tangle of prickly pears. And on she ran, the little hands clinched. Not far now; only the narrow path between the high rocks and the river.

She came to the end, and before her lay the plain, and the silver farmhouse. "Yes, I'll tell them," she said, "I am almost there!" Between her and the farm were three low figures moving over the low bushes; the short one, the one in the blouse, and the one in yellow. She sank down on the ground, with her injured hands before her, and she cried: "I cannot help them now! They are in the land of dreams from which they never will return!"

Righto, yes. . . Three things can happen. *(Smiling)* Well, it's a children's story, so anything can happen. First, she watched them and they burn the house to cinders and shoot the three Boers, and after a lot of indecision. . . she goes into Cradock and. . . finds the Englishman with the blue blouse and they spend all the money? Not at all, she's too young for that; I told you, she's only rising fourteen. . . *(As if in answer to the audience)* Well, she is. That would be immoral, yes. . . *(Contradicting)* No, I think she's quite unaware of an outside world. She'd want to stay with her goats in bondage.

Second: put on an extra spurt and just get to the farmhouse. Then the farmer shoots the Bushman and the Englishman in the blue blouse — with his wife handing him the cartridges — and the daughter comes out, and she and Henrietta wrestle with Dirk. And they get his bowie knife and stab him, just to teach him a lesson. And the farmer beats him and spares him, because good goatherds are hard to find. Dirk was all right basically; fell in with bad company. And Jannina, ach, is reinstated. . . and given her roaster-cake. Would that work? no, no?. . . And they put antiseptic on her hands, for pathos. No? Why not? — not true to life, all right.

Her father? No, he can't reappear; I told you, just a lump in the earth — she's been digging him up, confirming he's dead, for years! I'm a freethinker, and he really is stone dead. . . In one version of this story I made him, of all things, a Dane. A tribute to the original little cobbler, Hans Andersen. He's better as a half-white smous. Then you get the whole problem of allegiance; little Emilie really is an outcast; nothing is on her side. I'm tired basically of European stories recast to fit Africa; we must have some stories of our own.

So, what really happened? I'll tell you what Africa does to a girl like Johanna. *She just stood there screaming!* And the moonlight came down and the windmill creaked and she had to, had to waken them. To save her oppressors.

Now, the Boer's wife heard her first, and she got out of bed, fully dressed, but with a nightcap on her head, her face so. She's been sleeping very badly. She wonders if the stove is still warm. She wakes the farmer, but he rolls over and snorts. He's been dreaming too, of the Nagmaal, when he held his hat in his hands and sang to his God.

"Luister, pa," says Ma, "ik hoor iets. Ik wil net seker maak Petronella vrij niet met haar suitor nie."

"Nee ma," he says, "he's by the town, buying the cows we getting for her."

"Haai, pa," says Ma. "All you think of is cattle with lots of milk. But I'm sure I heard something crying, crying in the veld."

"Magtig," says the oom, "but you never let an honest man sleep."

But he did go out into the night with his gun.

The mother woke her fat daughter in the other room near the stove: "Wil jy nie 'n koppie koffie hê nie, mijn skat?"

"No, I also thought I heard something," she said. "I thought it was Hansie crying out for me. He didn't really want to go to town to buy cattle."

"Ag, my treasure," said Ma, "men, they all the same. They doesn' understand what a woman wants."

"I want him so long as he's good and true," said the daughter. "And then I can go to town too, and wear ribbons, and walk up and down Voortrekkerstraat, so."

"I have heard a strange thing tonight. Jou pa sê it was a jackal, but no jackal cries so. It was a child's voice, and it cried: 'Master, master, wake!'" and she handed her daughter a cup of coffee.

"Haai," said the daughter, "this coffee's full of grounds. 'Master, master, wake!' I also heard it so," she said.

And now they were truly frightened, and they made a great fire, and they sang psalms together all the while.

At last the farmer came back, and they asked him: "What have you seen?"

"Nothing," he said. "The goats is in the kraal and the moonlight is on the wall and the windmill is turning. And yet, it did seem to me," he added, "I saw three figures moving. And afterwards — it might have been fancy — I thought I heard the cry again, 'Master, awake, awake!' — but since that, all has been still." *(Pause; determinedly)*

Next day the navvy returned to the railway works near Ganna Hoek, where they're building the line from Middelburg. And his blue blouse was stiff with blood.

"Where have you been so long?" asked his comrades; they were all semi-convicts, forced labour.

"When he drank his grog today," said another, "he let it fall, and looked around." *(Pause)*

Next day a small, old Bushman and a run-away Hottentot in ragged yellow trousers — they were at a wayside canteen. When the Bushman had some brandy, he began to tell how someone. . . lifted up her hands and cried for mercy, how she kissed the white man's breeches and screamed for help. Then the Hottentot took the Bushman by the throat and dragged him out.

Next night the moon rose up and mounted the quiet sky. She was full now, touching the land with a weird and almost oppressive beauty. Her light caressed the willow trees, and the high rocks. . . all that I am leaving behind. And it fell on a little new-made heap of earth and round stones at Lily Kloof, South Africa. *(The story is over)*

It's the daughter I'm angry about, and the mother. Traitors, traitors! Can't hear a fellow creature's cry in the night.

(Straight into it: angry) I thought I stood in Heaven before God's throne, and God asked me what I had come for. I said I had come to arraign my brother, Man.

God said, "What has he done now?"

I said, "He has taken my sister, Woman, and has stricken her, and wounded her, and thrust her out into the streets; she lies there, buried. I am here to challenge him; that the kingdom be taken from him, because he is not worthy, and given unto me. My hands are pure." *(Holding them out)*

God said, "Thy hands are pure. Lift up thy robe."

I raised it; my boots were red, as if I had trodden in wine.

God said, "How is this?"

I said, "Dear Lord, the streets on earth are full of mire. If I should walk straight on them, my outer robe might be bespotted. Therefore I pick my way."

God said, "On what?"

I was upset; I let my robe fall.

"On the bodies of my sisters," I said, and I was ashamed. . .

That's another dream of mine. . . Some men must think the Almighty very ignorant, for they never kneel down to speak to Him without feeling themselves called upon to explain to Him the whole plan — of creation, the Fall and salvation — subjects on which, you might suppose, He would be better informed than they. And do you suppose they pray for their women; and do you suppose He notices the omission?

"There are two kinds of spiritual law, two kinds of conscience, one in man and another, altogether different, in woman. They do not understand each other; but in practical life the woman is judged by man's law, as though she were not a woman but a man." Not myself, but a man — Ibsen. I have yet, I have yet to find a woman with that understanding.

Now, where do we stand? I was telling you about Undine, who was taught to be good in a man's world.

"And what lesson does this teach us, my dear?" said the awesome governess.

(Getting on trunk) "That God has prepared a Heaven for the people He means to save, and a Hell for the people He means to burn."

"Hardly the right way of putting it, my dear. It teaches you that you should be a good girl, so that when you die God may take you up to Heaven, and not send you to Hell — to burn for ever and ever."

"I would much sooner be wicked and go to Hell than be good only because I was afraid of going there."

"Oh!" gasped the unfortunate governess, "what do you mean? You're always so evil and wicked."

"Yes, but not half so evil and wicked and cruel as He is. *(Raises fist and accusing finger)* Nothing is so evil, not even the Devil. The Devil is glad when we go to Hell, but he did not make us on purpose to send us there. I'm sorry for him, I believe he tries to be good and God won't let him. That's what I believe." *(Off trunk)*

And she stood there primly, like a carefully-brought-up Christian, receiving her Sunday lesson. Then she clasped her hands behind her and walked out of the room. The world was no place for her; why, then, had she been so bad and put in it? The Devil did not come to other people and make them think such thoughts. She felt very aggrieved by these attacks from the infernal regions.

(Passionate) She wished she was not a woman. I hate women; they are horrible and disgusting! I wish I had never been born rather than be one! Because it is an unpardonable offence against womanhood for us to entertain a thought — or give utterance to an idea — that has not been repeated till it's as stale as last year's loaf! You'll hear little in that line from me!

... Poor Jannita, poor poor Jannita...

She mourns ruefully, and resumes pacing, putting up her hair.
Fade.

3. October, 1889 — *Norham Castle* — London to Cape Town (Mode: Monologue)

I have learned things over here; experience is forced on me. About men and women, about the sex question. I have learned about — the way I am. I wanted to be a nurse, as you know, a doctor — but I am no good, no good at sums. Lacks application. All that's left to me is to be a writer! So I must tell you another story. It's called "The Nurse's Story." It's really about — the way things could have been for me. I'll tell it as I was told, in October, 1889, on the *Norham Castle.*

I am leaning over the side of the ship and turning back no wistful look at the English shores. England made me, and broke me. Like a great living creature, the steamer passes over the blue, breezy, swelling sea. We leave a track of foam and bubbles to dance and die in sunshine. The wild sea-birds dip their wings into the water and spread them in the morning light. It would be pleasanter to be among them — O sea-spirits —than among the wiser fowl on deck.

There sit two Afrikaner girls, right outside my cabin. They've been sent home for their education. Now they return, sublimely ignorant of everything in general, their own deficiencies in particular. They'll make great sensations in their up-country towns.

Further off is a portly dame wearing the stiffest black silks. She can't bring her eyes lower than her great gold rings. She used to do her own ironing, and her own washing, at a pinch, when no maid was to be got. Her husband has been a lucky immigrant; he stares at the rolling of the ship and longs to be in old Africa again. He returns smaller and wiser after his travels; he now knows the world has greater things than a British settler. His wife has had no such revelation, for the darkness that surrounds the female soul is dense.

A little to the right — stands a pimply young missionary, biting his nails. He is staring very hard at a very pretty blonde. She is going to the Cape to be married. A fish in the hand is worth six at the hook, and more than one bride has come to her beloved to find herself unwanted; so, if there are any golden fish on board, she might as well angle for them. Her eyes are resting, not on the palpitating missionary, but on smaller game — puny, white-faced Londoners, 'raw Englishmen' they will be called in the Colony — they will go into stores as clerks or become petty diamond-buyers at the Fields.

But the best are the children. Two with innocent blue eyes and dimpled faces, and masses of fine yellow hair. An ugly little terrier comes up to them; the smaller one gives it an astonishing kick.

"Oh Edith, how can you!" says her sister. "It belongs to that lady in the black dress."

"No, it doesn't, or I wouldn't have kicked it," says the little one. "It belongs to that woman with the plaited hair and the old grey frock."

"Oh, then it's all right," says the other.

Must one find the world, the flesh and the devil even in a morsel of humanity, not three feet high?

The woman with the plaited hair and grey dress is shabby, dreadfully. Her grey skirt has been turned, not only inside out, but upside down. Her loose cloth jacket, once black, is now brown. On her head she wears a great round hat; it must have been young when the jacket was black. She sits so nervously on the bench, as if she's not sure she has a right to be there. A boy with curly hair and a rich brown beard pats her dog, but when he sees her wizened face, he goes away. She gets up to store her dog in its quarters. I retire to my cabin to avoid them all.

Only later do I find that she is to share my cabin with me. It is better than having the captain's pretty sister or any of the other gay young butterflies. After the strain of the years, I can break down completely. She won't disturb me. In fact, she pays me silent, constant attention, sits beside me day and night.

"You are very good to me," I say to her, when I am lost and sweating, and she bathes my head with vinegar and water. "You do everything better than the stewardess."

She presses an apple from the dining saloon into my hand and smiles. She has such violet eyes.

She hasn't spoken for days, but this morning she says: "Are you going to someone?"

"Someone?" say I, "why no, I have no need of anyone."

"I beg your pardon," she says. "You look so happy when I brush your hair, and I thought you must be going to someone."

"No, I am alone," I say.

She waits for a long time, then says: "I have someone; I am going to him." She lays down her knitting and draws from her bosom an old gold locket, and puts it into my hand. And almost as an afterthought, she says: "He is dead now."

"Then why —" I say, "are you going to him?"

"To serve him. I never felt so before," she says, "but I would like to tell."

I stare at the locket with the young girl, pretty and weak, and the face of a man, a dark, handsome, sensual face with bold black eyes. I close my book and make a gesture that she should tell all. And she does.

"I was always so stupid," she says. "That was the reason nobody loved me. They sent me to school to see if it would do any good, but I used to get frightened. When we had to say our lessons, I could never remember. There was one teacher; I thought she loved me. But once she locked me in the cupboard, and she forgot me there, and I heard her telling the other teachers I was the stupidest girl in the school. I did so want someone to help me, someone bigger and cleverer than I was. Afterwards, I left off trying to make people love me. It was no use.

"When I was grown and wore long dresses my mother died, and my father after a little. So I had to go away from school, and I had only one aunt, a widow. She had a beautiful house by the sea, with a balcony and flower garden. She gave me a pretty green-and-white room all to myself, if only I'd teach the children and help her with needlework. So I used to get up very early and dress the children, and cook the breakfast. I used to work all day and late in the evening. When she used to ask me if I were not tired yet, I used to say no — because I wanted her to love me. Sometimes I went up to my room and just lay at the foot of my bed, crying myself to sleep. If she had sometimes looked at me as she looked at the children, I should never have felt tired.

"One day she told me she was expecting a friend of hers and her husband and child. They were coming to board with us; she was very delicate. And I had to move out of my room in with her children. It would give me more work, but I fancied perhaps — they would like me. She was a pretty woman and sat in the parlour all day. My aunt used to sit and talk with her. But she never took any notice of me. Her husband I was frightened of — he used to sit just outside the schoolroom window, and then I couldn't teach the children anything. I wondered how anyone could love him, till one day his own little girl sat there on his knee, and he looked down at her with such a look in his face. He was so strong that I ran away, that the children might not see me.

"After that, when I used to walk on the beach with the children and his little girl, he would often meet us when he was coming back from his bathe. He'd talk to his little girl and sometimes to me. He did not mind the other gentlemen seeing him talking to me, even though I always had my aunt's baby, and looked like a nurse-girl. He always talked so kindly to me. He said my arms were not strong enough to carry such a big baby, and I said, oh yes, they were.

"One day he brought a beautiful painting and hung it in the parlour. I was passing the door with a bottle for the baby, and he called me. 'Do you know why I bought it?' he said, 'because she looks as beautiful as you.' Then I felt him take my hand softly. I pulled my hand out of his, and ran to the children's room and cried, I was so happy. I never thought anyone would look at me as he did.

"In the evening two or three gentlemen came to play whist. My aunt told me to make some egg-flip. He had showed me how to make it, and I could, very nicely. But this evening he came into the kitchen, because he was afraid I would not do it right. We were all alone, and he put his arm round me and kissed my mouth. It seemed as if there were a great river running past my ears, and I sat down and put my head on the table. I did not think at all. It was all so strange, and I was so happy. I couldn't think because I was working, working all the time, with the children or at housework. At night I was so tired I couldn't undress, I went to sleep in my clothes... "

There the dinner-gong goes off, and I lie back and sure enough, she's back bringing me a pear.

"You look tired tonight," she says.

"It's the swell," I say. "Never mind."

By this time she has reclaimed the locket and hidden it in her portmanteau. It's the same old story, and you know how it goes from here. I have picked up her knitting and am following the pattern, three rows purl, three rows plain.

"Then," she says, "it was a Sunday night and I had time to rest and to think. They had all gone to church, and the baby was asleep. I could see his love for me was not like that for his little girl, or else why did he never kiss me when others were by? There must be something very wicked in it."

"It's always right to love," say I, "love as much as we can, and as long as we can, and as strong as we can."

"Do you really believe it?" she says. "Say it again."

"Say what again?"

"That it is not wrong," she whispers.

"Shelley and his wife went away from each other, and he loved another woman."

"But Shelley was a wicked man," says she, and she leans over and takes her knitting. "It's for my little dog," she says, "I am making him a doggy blanket."

By then it is spacious enough to embalm the little dog.

"Anyway," I say, "the Sunday night."

"The Sunday night I missed church," she says, and I wonder how many such services we haven't missed, there in our private cabin. We have missed the shuffle-board, and the bridge tournaments, and crossing the line. We're well into the southern seas of her story now.

"He had gone with the others to church, but just as I was thinking so, there he was, standing in the door. He came into the room and stooped down over me and asked what I was thinking. I told him it was wicked, and no one else would ever love me now. He told me there was nothing wrong in his loving me; he said some kinds of love were wrong, but he only loved me as if I were his little girl. He didn't show his love for me before others because his wife was so queer. She did not care for him at all; she did not like him even to have a man friend. He had never had anyone to love him, he longed for someone to, utterly. He asked me if I would not, for ever. Then I thought it was wrong of me to think I should not love him. He asked me to kiss him, and I did. Then I loved him better, and he called me his little sunshine.

"I felt incredibly glad and happy till the next day, when I was dusting the parlour. I heard his wife talking to him in the next room. 'I'm not a fool, not blind, either,' she said. 'I understand your games by this time.'

"I went out of the room then, because I did not want to hear more. But the thought came to me that they were talking about me. I asked him that evening, and he said: 'You must not mind her. It is only her nature. She'd be jealous of your aunt if you were not here.'

"Jealousy was something I had not experienced, but when I saw his wife taking his arm into dinner, I was jealous. When he played with his little girl whom I loved so much, and kissed her, I got a sick feeling at my heart. But he always called me his little sunshine, when we were alone. To me it was as if he were the only real thing in the world. I liked so to go and put his room neat, to touch the brushes he used every morning. One day his wife tore up his likeness, and I retrieved the pieces and put him in my locket there.

"One afternoon when it was fine enough for everyone to go to the beach, I was at home getting tea ready, and he came in. I was bending over the pantry dresser, filling a glass pot with jam. He lifted me down in his arms and carried me into the schoolroom which was all boarded up; we'd had terrible storms. Then he sat down with me on the chair, with me holding his neck. And he held me very close to him, and asked me if I truly loved him, better than anything else in the world. And I cried out loud, and he clutched his face to my ear and said, 'Then you must come away with me. To another land where we can be alone, together till we die.' And I cried, and his eyes were wet, and he did not let me go. And then I folded over, quite still for a long while, and he held me in his arms... Then I went to finish with the jam.

"After that day I loved him with another kind of love. I could not bear it when there were other people in the same room. It seemed as if they must see in my face how much I loved him. Once when he was away I took his greatcoat that hung in the passage, and slept under it. I didn't care if it smothered me in heat, so long as some part of him was with me. I'd sit on the schoolroom chair when the children were out, and feel the wooden frame and the stiff back, and touch the legs with my fingers. Do you think that was very stupid of me?"

"Well," I say, what else can I say? "Um," I say, casting around for a suitable aphorism. "If there were half as many responsible men in the world as unwanted children, Victorian England would be a better state!" Now she's been seduced; now she'll be abandoned. Apparently, thank God, there was to be no fatherless child. But imagine her on that school chair, wanting one, just to keep a piece of him. She was only a child herself, a stupid one; I agreed with her own estimation.

Then, to cut a long story short — and it is long; it lasts about to Table Bay, her telling me how she loves this Piece-of-Perfection, loves his hands, his boots, his hair — you know the style. She loves everything but the man whole, and he a faithless gadabout. O sister mine, what you do not know is that you love him only for what he calls forth in you; and what you do not tell me is where the real story lies.

"He wanted me, he said, when he carried me into the school-room, to love me forever. And he said he would leave his wife and child on my account. 'No, no, no,' I said, knowing how wicked that would be. 'No, no,' I said but he sat me on his lap in the chair, and said: 'Yes, yes,' he would leave them.

"I thought I must go and tell his wife, because I was the cause of his wickedness. One night I went to the door of her room, but the light was out, and when I stood close to the door I could hear her breathing, and his. I thought I must tell her that I was the source of everything evil in her life. But soon they were gone, and I never saw them again.

"After that I thought that if I laboured very hard all my life for other people, at work I did not like, it might make it right for him, a bit. I was very foolish, but that was my renunciation. I always hated to see blood and pain, so I got them to let me help in the Women's Hospital, and I learned to be a nurse. I'm very good at lying-in. At first I wanted to run away when I saw anything dreadful, but I knew it was helping, so I felt strong.

"I never heard of him any more. I thought he was tired of me before he went away, and that he would soon forget me. I thought so and for twenty years I never heard his name. But the other night I was sitting up with another old nurse. She was telling of a gentleman who hired her to go out to South Africa. I didn't really listen till I heard a name; it was his. She told me he had tuberculosis and must take a long voyage, but it did him no good.

"At last, one night in Africa, he opened his eyes and said: 'Come to me, come to me.'

"She asked if he wanted his wife, and he said, no, he wanted his little sunshine — those were his exact words. He did not say any more. And so I am going to him."

This voyage is almost ended. I sit with my companion on deck. Her blanket is big enough now to wrap herself and her dog. Presently she goes to feed it, only the best from the captain's table.

I watch the hot, bubbling sea, and the captain's sister walking up and down, with her arm on the arm of the handsome boy-man with the curly hair. He carries her great white hat in his hand and looks down at the little dark head beside him.

Fade.

4. 1891 — Cape Town
(Mode: Short story)

With a hat at hand and outdoor gear ready.
I have this old carved box. *(The lid is broken and it is tied with a string)* What travels it has been with me. In it *(Opening it)* I keep a little packet of paper with hair inside — my father's — my sister Ellie's; she died when she was three and I was ten, but this story is not about that. I keep in this box a little picture that hung over my brother's bed. Other things. I also have this — a rose. You also have such boxes, but none of you have my rose.

When my eye is dim and my heart grows faint, and my faith in woman flickers, and her presence is an agony to me — I feel that over men, too, as you shall see — the scent of this dead rose comes back to me. I know there will be another spring, as surely as the birds know. That is what it means to me.

There were other flowers in this box. A bunch of white acacia flowers, gathered by the strong hand of a man, when it had rained, and the drops fell on us from the leaves down my neck. The flowers were damp and made stains on the paper I folded them in; I threw them away. Flowers have much significance in my family; when my mother married my father with a wreath on her bonnet, the Rev Dr Campbell tore it off — frivolities were not for a missionary bride! But I have a faint smell of dried acacia that recalls that sultry summer afternoon, and the rose. I will tell you its story, as I have been writing it down.

It is twenty years now, when I was a girl of fifteen, and I went to visit my sister Alice, in Fraserburg, near Beaufort West in the Nuweveld. It was a four-day coach trip and I couldn't — eat. Once a lady handed round biscuits; I took one, but was unable to swallow it. At a hotel I saw a piece of cheese on the table and had an intense desire to — snatch it up and run away. When I got to my sister's, I was received very coldly. I started to eat, but the agony was so intense I rushed outside and flung myself on the ground; then they were kinder to me. There I also met Mrs Mary Brown and her husband, the district surgeon; they understood me better.

Fraserburg was also young in those days, and the population consisted mostly of men. A few, like Dr Brown, were married and had their wives and children; but most not. There was only one other young girl there when I came. She was seventeen, fair and fully-fleshed; she had rather heavy lips until she smiled.

The hotel-keeper may have had a daughter, some of the farmers had, but we never saw them. She reigned alone. She was the only woman all those single men had to think of. They talked of her on the stoeps, at the market and the pound; they watched for her at the streetcorner. They hated the man she bowed to or walked with down the street. They brought flowers to the front door, they offered her their horses, and when they dared they begged her to marry them.

Now, that is how men are — there was something noble and heroic in their devotion to the best woman they knew, while to their cooking girls they'd give all hell. Partly there was something natural in it; shut off from the world, these men must pour at the feet of one woman the worship that otherwise would have gone to twenty. Twenty women whom they'd have happily married and condemned to thankless drudgery for evermore. But partly there was something mean in their envy of one another. If she raised her little finger, I suppose, any one of them would have been at the others' throats.

Then I came. I do not think I was prettier; I was half starved, sickly. I don't think I was even as pretty. But I was vital, and I was new, and she was old — so they all forsook her and followed me! They worshipped me! Now the flowers came to my door; it was I who had twenty horses offered me when I could ride only one. For me they waited at the streetcorner; it was what I said and did they talked of. Partly I liked it. I had lived alone all my life, and no one had ever bothered to tell me (a) that I was beautiful and (b) that I was a woman. And — I believed them. I did not know then that it was simply the fashion for young masters to follow. I liked them to ask me to marry them, and to say, no, I am nobody's servant! I despised them. I was too young to be tender, and I liked my power. I was like a child with a new whip, not caring how I cracked it. I could make a man's face ring with blood and pain. Men were curious creatures who liked me; I could never tell why.

Only one thing took from my pleasure; I could not bear that they had deserted her for me. I liked her great dreamy blue eyes, I liked her slow walk and Colonial drawl. When I saw her sitting with men, she seemed to me to be too good to be among them. I felt sure she hated me — that she wished I had never come to the village — that she wished I was dead. She did not know, when I went out riding, and a man who had always ridden beside her came to ride by me, I sent him away. She did

not know that once when a fellow thought to win my favour by
ridiculing her accent — "Wagt een bietje, alles zal recht kom"
— I turned on him, so fiercely that he never came before me
again.

But I knew she knew that at the hotel men made a bet as to
which was the prettier, she or I; and asked each dude who came
in; the lout who staked on me won. I hated them for that, but I
would not let her see that I cared about what she felt for me. She
and I never spoke to each other. If we met in the only street of
Fraserburg, we bowed to each other and passed on.

At last the time for my departure for here, Cape Town, came.
I was to leave the next day. Dr Brown gave a party in my
honour. The entire village was invited. And it was midwinter;
there was nothing by way of flowers, only dahlias and chry-
santhemums — not a rose for love of money. Except in the
garden of a friend of mine — there was a rosebush, with one
bud. It was white... but it had been promised to the fair-haired
girl to wear. To her — she was to get it... *(Break)*

There's where I gave up on my story. *(Pulling on outdoor
clothing; gloves, parasol)* Now I am a woman of thirty-six, with
considerable experience in the affairs of men. Parliament, by
the way, is the same age as me. It's a winter's afternoon once
again, and I am tired of writing of things that never happen. I go
to the Lower House to see how the men are getting on. For the
second time they are debating the Masters and Servants Act.
What they want to do is substitute lashes for fines and impri-
sonment for minor offences. Shall I tell you what they are?:
absence from work; intoxication; riding a master's horse; dis-
obedience! This is also called the Strop Bill, and you must know
that Mr Rhodes votes for it. I call it the 'Every Man Wallop his
own Nigger Act.'

The seats were empty. In the front row of the Ministerial
Benches a man sat with his hat on and his chin upon his breast.
Next to him sat a man with one leg under him, who was fiddling
with a piece of paper. Beside him sat a dude with an eyeglass on
and his head thrown back... asleep. The next seat was empty.
Two of the men had gone to their afternoon tea. Another lout
was in the hall, whispering with his head close to a country
member.

On the opposite side a Bondsman with long hair, speaking in
the Taal, was making a fuss about the wickedness of kaffir
servants — how his wife had to light her own stove and fry his

sausages every morning. I leaned my head on the front of the gallery, wishing I'd stayed home and finished my story. I watched the gilt mace on the table, and the books, and the Speaker's wig.

Then, like one of the liberal members, I fell asleep, and I thought I was in heaven; and a crowd of men stood at the door. I was squeezed through...

Presently there was a knock at heaven's door. God said to the angel who kept it: "Who is there?"

The angel said: "John X. Merriman, my Lord."

God said to the angel who kept the books: "What is written of him?"

The angel turned over many leaves. "Mmm," he said, "I find he holds antiquated views with regard to woman."

God said: "Many men feel so, and most women deserve it. Anything more to the point?"

The angel turned over more leaves: "I find it recorded that he has a sense of humour."

God said: "We need more of that. Let him in!"

And the little door opened, and John X. walked in and made a great bow, removing his hat.

There came another knock at the door, and God said: "Who is it?"

The angel at the door said: "He says his name is Sir James Sivewright, my Lord."

God said: "I used to know him, but have not heard of him for ten years. What has he done with the intellect I gave him?"

The angel asked Sir James, and said: "Oh, Strop Bills, speculations... a man without an ideal."

God said: "Cape politics is too much personality and not enough principle. Take him away."

But a little voice piped up from some far corner of heaven: "Oh my Lord God, he was very kind to me." And another chipped in: "And to me, too."

God said: "Confirm if this be true."

The recording angel said: "Those are his servants' voices, my Lord; they loved him."

God hesitated, and the deep little voice far away wailed: "Oh save him, my Good Lord."

"All right," said God, "let him come in!"

And Sir James came in and took his seat in the second row, two seats from John X., and I was glad to see him there; I always knew it would be so.

Then another knocked on the door. God said: "Who can that be?"

The angel said: "He gives the name as Sir J. Rose Innes, my Lord." And the recording angel began to turn the pages back to I.

God said: "There is no need. I know him. Let him come!"

And the angel went down to get him, and he gave a huge bow to his master, and sat between John X. and Sir James, and they were like three brothers together.

There was another who had his head in the door; he had an eyeglass on. God said: "Tell him to take that thing off; he can see me without it."

The angel said: "It is J. W. Sauer, my Lord."

God said: "Read."

The other angel said: "There are many entries, some in his favour and some, alas, not. It stands that the man is opposed to the Strop Bill."

God said: "All men who oppose the Strop Bill are saved! Let him in!"

And Sauer tiptoed in, and took his seat besides Rose Innes, and he looked up at God with his chin in the air.

"Next," said God.

And in came Sir Pieter Faure. God told them to look him up in their books, where it was written that he went round South Africa making promises he never kept.

Sir Pieter Faure whipped off his hat and crumpled the brim in his hands.

God said: "All politicians make promises. There wouldn't be any in heaven if we let that count. Why should he be lost? Let him in, for goodness sake!"

Then we all went to tea.

We'd just got our cups full and little watercress sandwiches when we all heard a terrific noise at the door.

God said: "I know who that is — Cecil Rhodes, on whom the sun and moon must have set."

And the recording angel rushed back to the book and frantically turned the pages: "He's a — an upholder of the Strop Bill, and a very big Capitalist!"

God said: "That does it. Take him to hell!"

"Will you have a second cup?" said an angel, all dressed in gold. I myself dared say nothing as I was only there by an oversight. I quailed when I heard a horrible shout outside. It was all the devils in hell setting on him, as in a rugby scrum. They kicked him down and beat him all the way to hell.

God returned his cup and resumed his seat, ready to judge some more. But now there was a really great noise. It was all the devils in hell coming up again, flailing Rhodes with their tails. They crowded round the door, their mouths hanging open.

God said: "Why have you brought him back again? Didn't I give him to you to damn?"

"Oh Lord God," said the devils, "we tried to. We shoved and kicked him to the great front door, but he stuck fast in it. He is too large for it."

God said: "Why didn't you try the tradesmen's entrance?"

The devils said: "Lord God, we did, right where the gridirons turn in the kitchen and we render down fat. But he is too large for them to cope. We tried the hole outside De Beers, and the goldmine shafts, and even they can't take his size. It would have brought all hell down if we'd tried any further."

And God turned and said: "All right, take down that wall and bring my son here. There is no room for him anywhere in Rhodesia. Only heaven will do." And He made a place for him at the footstool.

And Rhodes walked up the steps with his hands behind him, and a smile on his face, just as when there is a division. That's how he crosses to the opposite side with all the House behind him.

Then God said: "Through grace you are here, not merit. Do you understand?"

And Rhodes bowed very deeply, touching his feet.

I thought I should slip out, for I knew I had no place there, but I looked back at God and at Rhodes. I saw all the Ministry sitting there. Their hair was combed down smooth behind, and do you know what? — they were singing a Te Deum.

The angel at the door winked at me and said: "With God all things are possible."

Then a policeman told me I was not to lean my head on the front of the gallery. I raised it, and looked down on the House below. John X. had indeed taken off his hat, and was contemplating it. Rhodes had moved his one leg from under him, and left off doodling. Sauer — Sauer still had his eyeglass on, and sat up, pretending he was awake. Rose Innes and Faure came in, and were wiping their lips. Sivewright was whispering to the country member. The Bondsman was still talking about his wife and the string of sausages; she must have been frying them one by one...

I went out to get a cup of tea at the Parliament Café in Adderley Street, and to walk in the glorious Botanical Gardens. So much for the world of men. *(Throws hat, umbrella, gloves off)*

And then I got back to my story of when I was in Fraserburg — and that wonderful evening of my party in the town hall. When I went to the waiting-room to take off my mantle, I found the fair-haired girl there, fair as an angel. She was dressed in pure white, and with her great pale arms and shoulders showing, and her hair glittering in the candlelight. The white rose was fastened at her breast.

I said: "Good evening," and turned away to the glass. I hated to look in it, because I never seemed to see myself. I arranged my old black scarf across my old black dress.

Then I felt a hand touch my hair. "Stand still," she said.

I looked in the glass. She had taken the rose from her breast. She was fastening it in my hair.

"How nice dark hair is, hey." She stepped back and looked at me. "It looks much better there."

I turned round. "You are so beautiful to me," I said.

"Ag," she said, "I'm glad you don't hate me." We stood smiling at each other...

Then they came in and swept us away to dance. All the evening we did not come near to each other, we had so many men to entertain. Only once, as she was doing the vastrap, she smiled at me.

The next morning I left Fraserburg. Recently I heard she did marry and went to America; it may or may not be so. But the rose — the rose is in the box to this day. *(She puts it there)*

When my faith in woman grows dim, and it seems, for want of love, of magnanimity, she can play no part in any man's heaven — then — then the scent of that pathetic withered thing comes back to me. For me it means — spring cannot fail us...
(She closes the box; houselights begin to come up)

Well... well, that's the story. Time for refreshment. Shall we prorogue before the next sitting? Etc. Thank you, thank you...
(Encouraging the audience to disperse)
Interval

PART TWO

5. December, 1913 — *Edinburgh Castle* – Cape Town to London
(Mode: Speech)

Lighted cigarette in one hand, mapping pen in the other, glasses on; standing at writing desk as at a podium, waiting for all to settle down; awkward but rhetorical.
Madam president, honoured members, ladies of the Lyceum Club, gentlemen guests, Mr Cunninghame Graham, Mr Jerome K. Jerome, honoured fellow members of the press, dear and honoured friends...

I am unaccustomed to banquets in my honour, here in Piccadilly at the heart of the world... but I am not unaccustomed to public speaking; I have been on the hustings in the cause of women for thirty years! I who, in 1882, struggled in the rain down Regent Street with a rejected manuscript of a novel, much rejected, an unpublished female novelist far from her native African farm... yes, what other forum was there open to me in those days but fiction?...
She takes a long draw on her cigarette; scrunges it out. Waits.

(Begins again in a new key) Madam president, honoured members, Mr Jerome...

Unaccustomed as I am to postprandial elaborations, and a very fine meal it was, too — I address everyone, kitchen maids included, skivvies and drudges of the Lyceum Club, here just off Piccadilly. I have said elsewhere, in my newly-published *Woman and Labour*, the culmination of my life's work as a sex researcher, "We claim all labour for our province, labour and the training that fits us for labour!"

In my early youth I began a book on Woman. I continued to work on it until ten years ago. It started by tracing the differences of sex function from the amoeba, yes, through evolution, to its highest aesthetic and intellectual plain: a point of development which the human race as a whole has not as yet reached — the age of the New Woman and the New Man.

When these chapters were ended, I went on with woman's condition in primitive societies; I had been watching the native African women about me — their child-bearing, their almost majestic attitude of acceptance of the inevitable, their self-sacrifice — I realised the women of no race or class will ever rise

37

in revolt, however intense their suffering, while the welfare and persistence of their society requires their submission. I felt that woman's suffering and weakness in child-birth, and in certain other directions... I lose one week in four — three days before, when I am high-tensioned and irritable, and then three days while it lasts I am stupid and want to lie down, and no one to be cross with me. It puts me into a madness. The battle is all within. It is as though my brain had blood there... I used to feel that way. Thank God that's over. That pain, that cramped, breathless suffering is the price woman has been compelled to pay for the passing of the race from the quadrupedal into erect status. Then — then I went into the physiology of women, and their relation to agriculture...

Next came what is more popularly known as the Woman's Question — with the causes which in modern European societies are leading women to attempt to readjust in their relation to society. I directed this both to the man who, in an instant of light-hearted enjoyment, begets the infant of the future, and to the woman, who bears it continuously for months within her body, and who gives birth to it in pain and who, if it is to live, is compelled to nourish it for months from the blood of her own being — and still who, as modern conditions develop, are thrown increasingly into the stream of economic life to sustain themselves and others by their own labour. Yet are they bound hand and foot, not by the physical and intellectual conditions of their own labour, but by artificial constriction and conventions, the remnants of a past condition of society like these ridiculous — ridiculous clothes we wear!

And it is a disease like a cancer that afflicts us that for equal work, equally well performed by a man and a woman, it is ordained that the woman — on the grounds of her sex alone — shall receive a lesser recompense. That is the nearest approach to a wilful and unqualified wrong I know of, in society today. I crush down my indignation on this point; I wish to maintain an impartiality of outlook.

But I maintain that sex and the sexual relation between man and woman also has an end entirely above the physical reproduction of humanity. That union has in it, latent, higher forms of creative energy and life-giving power, and its history on earth has only — only begun. As the first wild rose when it hung from its stem with its centre of stamens and pistils, and its simple whorl of pale petals, had only begun its course, and was destined, as the ages passed, to develop stamen upon stamen and petal upon petal, till it assumed a hundred forms of joy and beauty — *(Bends to add the words:)* And pistil upon pistil... *(She finds something that troubles her and, while lighting another cigarette, deletes whole pages. Then, after a deep breath, she resumes)*

(Vigorous, jaunty) Ladies and gentlemen of the Lyceum Club!

We now come to 1913, and we are approaching war — the most horrible war the world has ever known. In the Boer War the soldiers burnt that book I outlined for you. Never mind, I have another for this war!... But this be the point: if women ruled, there would be no war!

For today, we take all labour for our province, but what of war? That day when the woman takes her place beside the man in the governance and arrangement of the external affairs of her race will also be that day that heralds the death of war. What is war? Just a means of arranging human differences. For men it is a sort of dangerous football! I wish we women could run this country, because men always seek the gain of the moment and cannot look far enough!

No woman could look upon a battlefield, but the thought would rise in her: "So many mothers' sons! So many bodies brought into the world to lie there — with glazed eyeballs, and fixed, blue, unclosed mouths, and great limbs tossed — this, that an acre of ground might be manured with human flesh, that next year's grass or poppies, or milk-bushes, may spring up greener and redder where they have lain." And we cry: "This should not be!" No woman who is a woman says of a human body, "It is nothing!" This taking of life has no other name but murder! It is not her cowardice, or her incapacity, or even her superior virtue, that will end war; she knows the history of human flesh; she knows its cost.

Her knowledge is superior to that of man. Men's bodies are we women's work of art. Given to us power of control, we will never carelessly throw them in to fill — to fill up the gaps in human relationships made by international ambitions and greeds. The thought would never come to us as women: "Cast in men's bodies; settle the thing so!" No matter how just the cause. There are other methods. Arbitration and compensation would as naturally occur to us as cheaper, and simpler, better ways. This is an issue on which man and woman must stand at a somewhat different angle.

Besides, it is more easy to destroy than to create, have you thought of that? Women have that three-in-the-morning kind of courage. Do you realise that, even today, the probability is greater that the average woman will die in child-birth than that the average male will die in battle? Yes, it is our intention to enter into the domain of war and labour there till in the course of generations we have utterly extinguished it! *(She smokes; lights another cigarette from the last)*

(Casually) Friends, friends, good friends...

The Woman's Movement of today is not an abnormal growth. In the confusion and darkness of the present, it may well seem to some that woman, in her desire to seek for new paths of labour and employment — is guided by an irresponsible impulse. Our old fields of labour have closed up and are submerged behind us; we demand entrance into the new. Perhaps you think she seeks selfishly only her own good. But, when a clearer future shall have arisen, and the obscuring mists of the present have been dissipated, may it not be clearly manifest that not for herself alone, but for her entire race, has woman sought her new paths?

Let it be noted exactly what our position is, who today, as women, are demanding new fields of labour and a reconstruction of our relationship with life. For men, change has come, and left nothing as it was. On lands where once fifty men and youths toiled with their cattle, today one steam-plough passes swiftly. Time was when the size and strength in a man's legs and arms largely determined his power. Now, the puniest mannikin behind a modern Maxim gun may mow down, in perfect safety, a phalanx of heroes whose legs and arms a Greek god might have envied. The man who invents one labour-saving machine may, through the cerebration of a few days, have performed a labour it would otherwise have taken hundreds of thousands of his lusty fellows decades to accomplish. But our position is not that of the male unemployed; it is this:

We women have become parasites, cosseted on our divans like pugs. Even our minor domestic operations are passing out of the circle of woman's labour. In modern cities our carpets are beaten, our floors polished, for us. Most of us have only to lift the fork to our mouths to be fed. We, who once nourished and clothed and educated our young, have our garments made for us, and schools and universities take our children. What is there left for us to do, but depend on the slavery of the lower classes, and the length of our husband's purse; pampered, maintained, restricted to our reproductive function — prostitutes — I use that term in the broadest sense, to cover all forced relationships based on necessitous acceptance by women of material goods in exchange for the exercise of her sexual functions — prostitutes! — And, for the first time in the history of the world, that woman's role can become extinct! We want sex based, not on economic bondage, not on the crabbed, shut-in old world, but on spontaneous, clean, honest affection of the man for the woman and the woman for the man — a co-partnership between free beings.

And the freedom of the New Woman means the freedom of the New Man. On this point, it's not the attacks of my enemies that wear me out, but the half-hearted support of my friends... The New Man, yes, yes... For the first time in the history of the... it's a new century, it's not too late, it's... *(Breaking down, but pulling up sharp; blots out cigarette)* Let me put it this way:

The ancient Chaldean seer had a vision of a Garden of Eden, which lay in a remote past. It was dreamed that man and woman once lived in — once lived in joy and fellowship, till woman ate of the tree of knowledge and gave to man to eat; and that both were driven forth to wander, to toil in bitterness, because they had eaten of the poisonous fruit...

We also have our dream of a Garden *(Beginning to echo herself)*, we do. But it lies in a distant future, distant. We dream that woman shall eat of the tree of knowledge — together with men — with man, side by side, hand close to hand to hand, through ages of much mutual toil. They shall raise — raise about them an Eden — created by their own labour — made beautiful — beautiful — by their own — fellowship, wherein dwells — love — love of comrades, co-workers, and friends.

You future generations — will look back at us astonished — you will wonder at our passionate struggles — that accomplished so little — at the truths we grasped at — but could never quite get our fingers round — but what you will never know is — how it was — thinking of you — and for you — that we struggled as we did — that it was the thought of your fuller life, men and women — that gave us consolation — for the futilities of our own —

Here she seems to collapse internally; hunches over slowly into a chair, is blank for a while; then cries quietly to herself.

Fade.

6. 1903 — Cape Town to Port Elizabeth
(Mode: Song)

With an apron over her dress.
   Hugging a mierkat to her cheek; singing:
        O 'Alliet, O 'Alliet
        A mierrie kat, a mierrie kat, a miler —
        How fat you get, how fat you get
        A mierrie kat, a mierrie kat, a miler —
        O none can touch, none can touch
        A mierrie kat, a mierrie kat, a miler —
        I love you much, I love you much
        And you belong and you belong to Empie Schreiner —
(Puts the pet down) Oh, isn't that a biggy biggy cabin floor-floor for lickly 'Alliet and her brood? Tchoo tchoo tchoo — and uppies dla tlunk — and underneath da bunk, no, huppies huppies — 'Alliet, huppies now, don't be shy... That's my girl. Now — no, you stay dere, that's my 'Alliet... Now, where's aTomalins? You don't know, you must know — he can't have got out, dere's a bigga bigga hatch and it's a special design to stop mierries being swept overboard.

Under the washstand — ah, come boy, a Tommy boy, come come *(Whistles)* No, you don't you — always trying something, never a dull... *(Grabs him)* aTomalins, aTomalins a Tiler — loo kleep to lourself, loo explorel ooh *(Hugs)* and stay wid dyour mummikins.

Now where's Itty-von... Ittytyty... oh, Itty-von'z ee goodee von and besty-von and sweetest-von and clever — so clever, Itty's my bitty, pretty city-von. You're always so obedient... And now? Dere you are.

Where's Inbred-Sin? Where indeed is Inbred-Sin? Not under the chair, and not under the bunk, and not under the washstand, and not under the writing desk. *(Opens portmanteau)* And there is Inbred-Sin. Qvicky qvick do da fambily — group photograph, group photograph. Smiling, smiling, *Click* - and we send it straight to the chemist. And now —

What — what are you going to tell the captain when he comes on his rounds — what are you going to say? Now I'll tell you. First you introduce yourselves — you say:

I am 'Arriet, 'Alliet are you listening, and I belong to Olive Schreiner and — these are my brood. You got that — my brood. And — I am 'Arriet's son, and I am called Tommy de

Wet — now you know that, don't you? Tommy a Tomalins, and they call me De Wet because I'm difficult to catch. And —

I am called Itty-von, which means Little One and I belong to Olive Schreiner and I am actually the cleverest one because size is not everything. And —

I am Inbred-Sin and I needn't explain. Right —

Now all together — say Thank You to the nice captain for letting you on board — say —

Oh you don't, you don't — tell him the story about the dominee. The dominee comes on huisbesoek and you take such an instinctive dislike to he won't have any cricket on Sundays and you go for him, savage him and you've got him in the corner with skirt shooing *Voertsak voertsak!* No — I don't think the captain, not to the captain...

Ready for inspection!

Now... *(They disperse; resigned)* oh, oh... Mierries gotti play-play Monopoly, all right. Do not pass Go. *(Skipping in a square)* One tloo tlee... Take a tram to Eloff Street. One two... go to Cape Town station... Three four five... Maitland cemetery, can do without that. Six seven... own a hotel in Aliwal North. Eight nine ten... Go to Jail. Just visiting... No, you *cannot* pass Go without a whole reward...

Oh gone, you're hopeless players, gone gone gone... I give up.

(Elated, she scoops up Tommy; cradles him)

        O Tomalins, O Tomalins
        A mierrie kat, a mierrie kat, a miler —
        Forgive my sins, forgive my sins,
        A tommy kat, a tommy kat, a tiler —
        I love you much, I love you much,
        A tommy kat, a tommy kat, a tiler —
        And none can touch, and none can touch
        'Cause you belong and you belong to Empie Schreiner.

Fade.

7. January, 1897 — *Dunvegan Castle* – Cape Town to London
(Mode: Letter)

Seated in her cabin; shuffling letters.
I have, all my life, lived in such solitude from my kind that I
have sought to bring them closer to me by — writing letters. If
I'd contented myself with less personal forms — fiction, alleg-
ory, pamphlets... if I'd stuck to those, there'd have been a
dozen novels, hundreds of allegories, oh pamphlets on scores of
issues. But a letter, written to one true friend, for me takes as
much art, and conveys as much feeling. The telephone is no
substitute. A letter is like a gift — a personal one, designed to be
the receiver's delight.

I have said many hard things against the British, but who can
decry their Royal Mail services? This ship, which already has a
hold full of my letters, is our six thousand mile lifeline. I have a
routine; on the homebound voyage, I write back to South
Africa up to Madeira — that gets my chores done. From
Madeira I write forward, bearing them myself to the red lips of
Her Majesty's postboxes. Now, this is done quite systematically; see, I keep a copy in case I am misquoted, or cannot
remember. Then I write out in fair, seal, expedite.

Dunvegan Castle
before Madeira
10 January 1897

Dear Will,
An Englishman is like a Jew; he seems to be either Christ or
Judas. But on the whole, much as I love all races of men, I think
we do pretty well — not better than other races, but we have our
peculiar virtues as we have our vices. The worst type of English
man or woman is the most canting hypocrite that ever lived —
the earth produces nothing lower. But — then there is some
corner of the English nature that produces a curious power of
sacrificing all for humanity, a curious power of obliterating
self-interest. Take the present Transvaal business — there are,
even in the Colony, a number of purely English men and
women, who love England passionately, but are throwing all
from them, self-interest, national feeling, and are willing to
expend their all in the Transvaal cause. I have to keep my head
down here — that arch scoundrel, your dear Mr Rhodes, is in

the next cabin. Yes, if I meet him on the hurricane deck, I just
scuttle past. I have *Trooper Peter* in my portmanteau, and it'll
do more damage to him — and to me — than a Maxim gun. I
hope you'll be able to stand the shock in your career.

I wonder if the Lord has spoken a curse out over us Schrei-
ners that we should be evil for the things we love best. Fred,
Ettie, I, you, we are all the same... But, I tell you, the Boer
republics are the last sluice gates before the Capitalists flood
the world. If it is necessary to pull down the whole structure of a
society to get out that stain of greed that lies at the foundation
of it, it must be pulled down, and built up again better! I can do
no otherwise — God help me and you! Amen!

Matjesfontein
15 April 1890

To Havelock Ellis,
Harry, you don't know what Philistines the people in Africa
are. I think if I lived fifty years in Africa I should never have one
friend. I can understand how bitter I used to feel against human
beings, and how I hated them, and felt myself utterly alone
among them, and only liked the Boers and Natives. Fancy a
whole nation of lower middle-class Philistines, the hardest and
narrowest hard-shell Philistines that God ever made, without
an aristocracy of blood or intellect or of muscular labourers to
save them! People here think anyone is mad who supposes that
one could perhaps think anything nicer than a great deal of
money. South Africa is quite eighty years behind Europe, and a
century behind Australia and New Zealand...

I'm getting faint with waiting for my dinner: this is a karoo
plant. The plants and the red sand seem like living things to me.
I like to touch them. When I wake up in the night, I think I shall
see them next day. They are the only things I feel near to in
Africa, and the blue sky and the stars. I like the ants too, and
the little mierkats. I could never love other nature in Europe as
I love this. Good night again. Your little Olive.

Matjesfontein
16 May 1890

Oh Havelock, I wonder if my work is good. I know it's all true
that I write, but I think what I write seems to become less and

45

less popular... I should like to get married now. It's very curious, but I could now. It wouldn't impinge on my individuality too much. No one could reach me now; you know what I mean. I know I shan't marry, but now for the first time in my life I feel that I could marry. But I have also given up the thought of ever finding a human being I could so love and look up to that I could marry him. Now that I expect so little from any personal relation, I could marry safely — there would be no disappointment...

30 July

To Havelock Ellis,
Boy, I am sending you old Chapman's letter to me. His two years' right to *African Farm* ends at the end of this year. This letter is all the hold I have of him in black and white. Will you try to arrange with him for another two? — he gave me £100 for the last two. Get this from him for the next, more if you can.

4th November

I have the most extreme humbleness with regard to my business faculties. I could command a fleet, govern an army, lead a nation, write an epic, sooner than make a bargain about seven-and-sixpence. I've about as much head for business as a cat!

I'm hopeless, I give all my money away. Do you know what I did with the payment I received for those anti-Rhodes articles — forwarded it to my poor little mother. Do you know what she did with it? — donated it to a fund to erect a statue in honour of Cecil Rhodes in Bulawayo!

Matjesfontein
26 September 1892

To T. Fisher Unwin
Sir, I insisted on *African Farm* being published at one shilling because the book was published by me for working men. I wanted to feel sure boys like Waldo could buy a copy, and feel they were not alone. I have again, last year, at the request of my publisher, allowed it to be printed at 3/6 as I felt sure most poor lads would have it within reach. *Dreams* is not published by me with the special intention of reaching the poor. I would prefer

46

the rich to have it. If I dedicated it to the public, I should dedicate it "To all Capitalists, Millionaires and Middlemen in England and America and all high and mighty persons." Therefore, except for a very large sum I will never sell the copyright, nor any right except that of printing it during my pleasure!

February, 1893

Dear Cronwright,

This is the little note I carried in my breast in an envelope, the day we went up the mountain near Buffel's Kop, to give you, but I hadn't the courage as I carried it down again. That day was so beautiful to me. It is very good one should once have had such beauty and joy in one's life as my first meeting you. Yes, it is curious how like Waldo you are; I have a curious, curious sort of feeling — that you are part of myself.

P.S. You are mistaken in feeling I have any special affection for the Native of this country. Our Labour Question does not materially differ from the Labour Question all over the world. Simply, what do intellect and power owe to ignorance and weakness?

P.P.S. I have the photo of you with that half-wild cat in your lap, and you look so solemn, and your hands are so strong.

Dear Cron,

The real question in South Africa is the Native Question... I would have given much if you and I could have spent days together and discussed this matter... There is something I can give you and I must try to give it in my letters. We must not meet again.

My darling Cron,

All possibilities are in your beautiful face, choked. The enemy we have to fight, the land we have to rule over, is not any poor Native; it is our *own strong passionate* dominating selves! Even physically, we have to hold ourselves fast. I do not dare to give way to feelings of any kind; if a man has a wild unbroken horse he must keep the bridle on him. Our passions are stronger than other people's... But I made up my mind when I was quite a little child that as soon as I was able I would support myself. I

47

see no reason why a woman should be dependent on her friends, any more than a man should. As long as I am well enough I shall support myself!

Oh Cron,
It's a strange thing that on Friday night, when you were at the Congress in Grahamstown, I woke up in the middle of the night and found I was sitting up on the side of my bed, crying and wringing my hands. It seemed to me something horrible had happened to you; I don't know what. I was crying so loud that everyone in the house must have heard me.

Last night was even funnier; it came on just as I was dropping to sleep, and for hours this kind of half-sleeping half-waking anguish lasted...

Yes, John Stuart Mill laboured for the Freedom of Women. But he did more. He laboured for Human Freedom. Many women have the vote — all will have it soon. If we wish to use our power to its noblest end, we shall have to learn the lesson Mill taught, that the freedom of all human creatures is essential to the full development of human life on earth. Liberty is indivisible. We shall have to labour for every subject race and class, and for all suppressed individuals. It's strange how very fond we are of freedom for ourselves, and how little we desire it for other people! Right and truth do prevail in the long run. I have been young; now I am so-so, but I've not seen a lie succeed. That's what I pin my faith to.

My Pal,
Our little baby was born at quarter past twelve on the morning of 30th April, 1895. I was put under chloroform and became insensible at a quarter past eleven. We had the best doctor and the best midwife. You were in the room throughout. When I became conscious at half past three in the afternoon she had been born a couple of hours. She lived that night. The last time I heard her cry from the other room was at quarter to four. When I woke at nine you told me she was dead. I want her buried with me. I'm sorry. With tender love, Your Brakje.
(Looks up; Cron is knocking at the cabin door.)
Cron, is that you?... oh yes... what's on the menu?...*(Repeating after him)* Soupe souveraine... Grilled trianon... Aspara-

gus à la Turque... Crêpes Florentine... my, Chicken à la Provence or Boeuf Russe... Bavarian cream... Coffee will be served in the lounge... Isn't there anything in English? Biscuits and cheese, no. Tell the captain — it sounds so good I feel I've had it already... Yes... *(Between her teeth)* Go away. *(Pulling forward a letter)*

You will perceive from the superscription above that I am still in 'Hell', otherwise known as Johannesburg. I have not written to anyone since I came here, because I have had nothing to write about but Johannesburg. It has crushed all power of thinking or feeling about anything else out of me.

You know the place, but I think only a woman's eye can be opened to all its hideousness. It is the women who are the most terrible thing here. Doubtless the mass of ill-gotten wealth obtained without labour and squandered with recklessness is the true source of the evil. It attracts the worst class of white woman to Johannesburg, and it demoralises those who were not demoralised before. But I don't mean it is the poor outcast women who are most terrible in this hell; it is the apparently respectable women. I have lived in Monte Carlo, London, Paris... I have worked among the outcast women and drunken sailors in the East End. But I have never seen anything so appalling, so decayed... In Johannesburg the whole moral fibre has relaxed...

I do not believe that just sexual degeneracy is the root of our evil in hell. We are a city given over to lust. Lust of money, lust of pleasure, lust of excitement, and the tone of our sexual morality springs from this general attitude. It seems to me hopeless to labour at the effect while the cause remains. Johannesburg, Johannesburg, you are sunken... *(Drops letter)*
Take me away, take me away, Cron...
(Sits and begins a letter)

Dunvegan Castle
20 January

My dear Mary,
He's a good man. But with marriage begins a woman's insight into the tragedy and bitterness of woman's fate and her deeper emotional life. Her broad intellectual life, as the free human creature's, dies with it — in all but a few cases.

I've had three miscarriages since the baby. It's curious how much I want that child, the one that died. It comes over me in fits as if I could go looking for it everywhere...

I think the life has been so terrible and intense since the Jameson Raid that I could not write of it to any human being. I have been cut off. When one is young, and especially unmarried, one seems to come closer to friends, because we can open all our hearts to them, and the one or two nearest and dearest of them can share all your life with you. Afterwards, life becomes so complex that the whole personal life must be lived quite alone in silence. To perfect strangers you can write and speak more easily; but to those you really love it is hardly worth expressing yourself unless it can be from the depths of your life. And so, you don't express yourself at all.

We're past Madeira now. This will reach you only just before I do. My regards to Dr Brown. I hope you'll like my new book; it promises some interest. All I want written on my grave is: "She wrote *Trooper Peter Halket of Mashonaland.*" Who cares for Rhodes, anyway? You'll see how he hangs the natives, and I'll hang him! He's right in the next cabin; I think I will cough and retch a bit, to make him think I'm ill.

Your ever-loving
Olive Schreiner.

Fade.

8. October, 1887 — London to Basle Express
(Mode: Journal)

Isolated; pencil on a page in her journal. With rising hysteria.
I am here — alone on the express train — alone with a terrible Frenchman! He is mad! He means to attack me! I am going to throw this journal out of the window if he does that someone may find it! My address is: c/o New College, Eastbourne, England! I am going to Pisa, the leaning tower! We do not stop again until the border! The St Gotthard Tunnel first! This will be terrible night to me, even if nothing happens!

He is sitting opposite me now! He is trying to put his foot against mine! He wants to wrap my rug around him and put my hat on! I dare not speak to him lest he should fly at me! I have never seen such a face — handsome, but with the awful look of one of the men in Balzac! He has his eyes fixed on me; I dare not look up or leave off writing! I've never felt such horror of any human creature! There's not any kind of bell to pull! Oh God, if the train would stop! There ought to be things of some kind to pull!

He turns away to rub the glass of the window! We are passing nothing! He is watching my reflection! I hate Frenchmen; if he were English I could talk him out of it! He's a tall slight man, fearfully strong! His hands can hold me like a child! We are passing Aix-la-Chapelle! He has just caught hold of my hair! He says he always thought English women wore bands! Oh God oh God what do I do? He is taking hold of my cloak and presses his face up to mine, and says he likes me and puts his hand on my thigh! *(Shaking head violently)* Non, je comprends pas Francais! Arretez! Arretez!

Perhaps we stop and he will have to get out! The minute we stop, out I leap! I have opened the window and am sitting by it that if he touches me further I can leap out! Oh, the tunnel, the tunnel! Stop! Stop! Stop!
The stage is plunged into blackness.

9. August, 1920 — *Balmoral Castle* — London to Cape Town
(Mode: Conversation)

Her terrible, choking, asthmatic breathing.
  *The lights come up dimly on Schreiner hunched with her back
to us in her long night-dress, hair undone, one sleeve pulled up.
She is just secreting away her medical apparatus and, as her
breathing begins to subside, turns, rolls down her sleeve and flexes
her arm. We see her as a ravaged, cumbersome, slow-moving
animal, painfully shaken but relaxing.*
  The phone (imaginary) rings and she lumbers across to it.
Mrs Schreiner... yes, please put him through. *(Gasping)* Oh
Pal, oh Pal, thank God you phoned... bromide of potassium,
chloral, amyl nitrate, digitalis, strychnine, now the opium. Is it
any wonder I cannot work, don't ask me?... I don't mind
death, my love, I am not afraid of it. But what's so terrible is
silence. You can't get a word across; not one. Don't disconnect!
  (Listening, panting) Yes, I'm the last of the Old Brigade.
Cron — for this old trouper life has become... one long struggle
for a cupful of air. All life seems to me... one long mistake: if
only once before I die... I didn't have time to explain to you...
it flashes on me... it was best so... It's strange... it's not the
wrong things in your life... that seem to have been the mis-
takes... but the things you did... most striving to do right... It's
such an intricate puzzle... it distresses me... Last-of-the-Old-
Brigade Last-of-the-Old-Brigade... *(Listening and smiling)*
  ... brings back to me that glorious time... when Socialism
was dawning... and we were all fighting... for full day... just
over the next hill... It does lie over the hill... but the day is
hot... it takes the race a long time, climbing... yes, cover up,
cover up... I have never had any doubt, my Pal, the day will
come... *(Grabs shawl)* Do you remember when... we went to
that protest meeting, and... they were shouting, "Three groans
for Olive Schreiner!" ... and you held my hand... But Socialism is only half the truth; the other half is individualism.
  Yes, I know, but it's hard... to work... I mean, now... a
needle goes through my heart when I look at my portmanteau... all unfinished... No Cron, no Cron, it is not death we
have to fear... it's the years of struggling... when the power has
gone! Yes, quarter-of-a-grain, quarter! Not half!
  Nothing surprises me... I feel so hopeless about the future
treatment of the Native... a little more, a little less makes no

difference... We will pay for it... but that doesn't prevent the wrong being done in the first place... Innocent persons will pay... Never the ones who actually did the wrong...

No, *no biography:* put down just this: I am a *one adult one vote man*... I believe that every adult inhabiting a land... irrespective of race... of race... sex... wealth... property... should have the vote, Cron. They don't need to know more about me than that. Are you there?...

(Puts down receiver, mumbles) Goodbye, my own sweetheart... It's not been easy... has it?

(Flexes her arm, gathers shawl comfortably about her) I suppose one never kills out one's passionate instincts... till death comes and sets one free... The terrible thing will be... if death comes and... instead of rest... the struggle goes on on the other side...

(Angrily raises her fist at the Almighty, one finger accusing) Old tyrant! We'll arrange things much better, you and I!... But I've not been working again. I'm in that wild restless state... I must 'shove on'. There is nothing helps like travelling when in pain... ach, just keep moving on, moving on...

God, if only you would let people die when they can't work and are no use... I seem to have my face to a wall without any opening... the portholes are all open, we're casting off... There it goes, the rumble of the anchor...

(Breathing deeply but more easily; to the audience) Do you want to hear some Emerson, then?... "Embosomed in beauty and wonder we are, in cheerfulness and courage, and the endeavour to realise our aspirations... The life of man is the true romance... which yields the imagination a higher joy than any fiction... Shall not the heart which received so much trust the Power by which it lives?... May it listen to the Soul that has guided it so gently... secure that the future will be worthy of the past?"

(Long calm silence; gently and fragmented) Africa, O Africa! I never knew how I loved you till now... I always see your blue sky... and your sky-blue mountains... and your red sand, wet with the blood of your own children...

A good, first-class deck cabin, otherwise I will not live through the voyage. But my heart, that travels third-class...

It's the fashion doctors have adopted... If they don't know what's wrong with you, they take out all your teeth...

No, a young man's love is not selfish... not like an old

married man's . . . he makes love to a younger woman and then forgets her in four weeks, four months, entirely. . . When I was just fourteen. . . a young man was very much in love with me. . . He asked me to marry him. . . I wasn't attracted to him; I said so. . . Yet after forty years when I was married and he was married. . . we were travelling on the same train. . . My husband and he often met and talked. . . But he and I never spoke, till the train was delayed somewhere. . . To pass the time the passengers got out and walked about. . . On the railway track were some tiny flowers growing. He picked three. . . and came to the window and put them in. He said: "You used to like wild flowers once!". . . He turned away, without another word. . . No elderly man who made love to a woman would keep as much feeling for her. . . even for ten years, one year, or for a day. . .

(With resignation and steely passion; clearly spoken)
    Give back my dead!
    They who by kop and fountain
    First saw the light upon my rocky breast!
    Give back my dead,
    The sons who played upon me
    When childhood's dews still rested on their heads.
    Give back my dead
    Whom thou has riven from me
    By arms of men loud called from earth's farthest
        bound
    To wet my bosom with my children's blood!
    Give back my dead,
    The dead who grew up on me!

Olive Schreiner, the gifted authoress, often found she needed a nerve and tissue builder. Read what she says about Sanatogen, the Food-tonic: "Sanatogen's effect upon me has been most remarkable. Nothing that I have taken for years has given me the same sense of vigour and restored circulation that Sanatogen has done. I shall try never to be without it". . . Did you get the cheque for my endorsement, Cron?. . .

All the streamers, and the farewell band playing on the quay, bomb-craters and wounded, concentration camps, King Edward gone too, the Boers gone, my family gone. . . my baby gone. *(She cradles her arms)*

Ach. . . *(Resigned but irritated)*, ach, ach, ach.

I love music and I love science; I love poetry and I love

practical labours; I like to make a good pudding and see people
eat it; and I like to write a book that makes their lives fuller. I
can do very little, and have never been so situated that I could
do my best — but I can live all lives in my love and sympathy!
All that is sad is that life is short and one can live so little of its
beauty oneself.

The streamers thrown in farewell tear. The band disappears.
Six thousand miles to home. Like a great living creature, the
ship pulls away from the land. The seagull's wing. Five thousand miles... four, three thousand miles, two thousand two
hundred, two thousand and one, two thousand, one thousand
and ninety-nine, ninety, eighty, sixty, twenty, nineteen, eight-
een...

Her eyes are closed; head sideways.
She breathes tranquilly.
Fade out gently.